Ten Things About

Pornography
&
God's Grace to Husbands

Ten Things About

Pornography
&
God's Grace to Husbands

Reggie Weems

Unless otherwise noted, Scripture quotations are taken from The Holy Bible, English Standard Version® (ESV®) Copyright © 2001 by Crossway, a publishing ministry of Good News Publishers. All rights reserved. ESV Text Edition: 2016

Copyright © 2018, Reggie Weems
www.10thingsabout.org

All rights reserved. No part of this book may be reproduced, scanned, or distributed in any printed or electronic form without permission.

First Edition: 2018

ISBN 978-0-9996559-2-4

To buy quantities of this book at a special rate for bulk use, email
info@greatwriting.org

Great Writing Publications
www.greatwriting.org
Taylors, SC

Table of Contents

   About the Series and this Book 9

   Introduction 11

1 There is Hope 13

2 It All Starts with God 19

3 The Truth about Sex 23

4 Spiritual Transformation 31

5 Ten Things about Pornography 37

6 Questions and Answers 55

7 Practical Pointers 67

8 Action Review Checklist 77

9 Conclusion 83

   About the Author 87

For husbands pursuing holiness

&

For wives who love them

About the Series and this Book

TEN THINGS is a series of books offering biblical encouragement and practical direction on matters of concern to modern Christians who are seeking Bible-saturated, Christ-centered, Spirit-empowered, practical guidance. The series is published in an electronic and print format for quick, private, and easy access.

The books are brief and to the point, enabling readers to access immediate help and genuine hope for real-life situations. They are also written in a pastoral tone intended to shepherd hearts and minds toward Christ-centered, whole-life transformation.

This encouragement is not intended to and cannot replace personal pastoral counsel or the accountability of living transparently in Christian fellowship with other believers. Both are invaluable to you. A particular book may inspire a reader, but lifelong change only occurs in the context of living in biblical community.

Because of its biblical and simple approach, pastors may also employ the series to disciple church leaders who minister to God's flock.

Introduction

*You shall love your crooked neighbor
With your crooked heart.[1]
(W.H. Auden)*

This book is an expression of love from one crooked-hearted neighbor to another, written by a self-confessed "foremost" sinner (1 Timothy 1:15). We are called to preach the gospel to ourselves and admonish each other (Colossians 3:16), to "encourage one another and build one another up…" (1 Thessalonians 5:11) as beggars telling one another where to find bread.

It is essential you experience this book as a primer, a first-word about the issue. It is not intended to create a long-term strategy for overcoming pornography and it's not a substitute for long-term counseling and accountability. Everyone needs incarnational, personalized ministry that is particular to him and his life situation.

---

[1] Authur C. Kirsch. *Auden and Christianity* (New Haven: Yale University Press, 2005), 16.

1

There is Hope

Pornography is adultery. It is inexcusable sinful behavior with uniquely damaging consequences. If you try to make excuses for it you will undermine your opportunity for freedom. Its horror is witnessed by God's use of the term *adultery* to describe unfaithfulness to himself. You have an idea of what pornography has cost you but the price is more than you presently know. Sin cost Jesus his life. It killed the person who loves you most. That's the horror of sin in general and of pornography in particular.

By its very definition, the gospel is good news rooted in the bad news of sin and its eternal consequences. Sin is the bane of human existence. It "condemns all men" (Romans 5:18) to a death (Romans 6:23) from which only omnipotence could rescue us. Pornography is sin but all sin is forgiven in those who repent of it and trust in Jesus for righteousness. The bad news is shockingly bad but the good news is incomparably good;

it is "grace greater than all our sin."[2]

The death burial, resurrection, and exaltation of Jesus assures us that "where sin prevails, grace abounds all the more" (Romans 5:20). The cross forgives and enables us to live beyond sin's putrefying grip. Like Lazarus called from the grave, the death-defying gospel calls us, resurrects us, and frees us to new life. It is "the power of God for salvation to everyone who believes" (Romans 1:16). That salvation doesn't only save you from God's eternal wrath; it enables you to daily live out its truths, inherently empowered (Philippians 2:13) with the divine promise that "he who began a good work in you will bring it to completion at the day of Jesus Christ" (Philippians 1:6).

Christianity is rooted in the realized hope of Genesis 3:15—the promise that Christ will crush sin and eradicate its effects. This is a cosmological and universal eventuality. Until then, it's also a practical reality as the Holy Spirit transforms Christians into the image of that perfect person, Jesus. In effect, Christianity is the expression of Jesus' life and not the repression of your sin. Salvation and sanctification are of grace and not of our works, although we must cooperate with God's grace.

In Matthew 19:28 Jesus claimed to be cre-

---

[2] From the song titled *Grace Greater Than Our Sin*. *Copyright*: Public Domain

ating a "new world," *palingenesias* in the original Greek. That term is used in only one other place in the Bible. In Titus 3:5-6, Paul wrote "he [Jesus] saved us…by the washing of regeneration and renewal of the Holy Spirit…" The English word "regeneration" is the same Greek word *palingenesias* of Matthew 19:28. What does it mean? It means that God is creating a new people for a new world—a people conformed to the image of Jesus, the prototype for us all (Romans 8:29).

There is hope that you can live free of an addiction to pornography because Christ has defeated sin in the power of his cross. His resurrected life is yours. As Paul succinctly stated, "For if while we were enemies we were reconciled to God by the death of his Son, much more, now that we are reconciled, shall we be saved by his life" (Romans 5:10). His death saved you. His life will sanctify you. This does not mean you will be perfectly free of temptation which will exist as long as we live in these finite, fallen bodies. But it does mean that you can live a life that loves God and others more than you love sin. As you might imagine, such salvation begins the same place the Bible starts, with God.

THINK ABOUT IT

There is hope that you can live free of an addiction to pornography because Christ has defeated sin in the power of his cross.

2

It All Starts with God

It may seem oxymoronic but the secret to overcoming sin is to focus on God and not the sin. In 1677, Henry Scougal wrote a letter to a discouraged friend. In it he states, "The worth and excellency of a soul is to be measured by the object of its love.[3]" Simply put, attention to and affection for Jesus makes our souls excellent. A focus on sin or ensuing sorrow depresses our soul. Thinking on Jesus elevates our soul.

Christianity begins and ends with God who reveals himself as "the Alpha and the Omega, the first and the last, the beginning and the end" (Revelation 22:13). Jonah painfully learned, "Salvation belongs to the LORD" (Jonah 2:9). It is in Jesus' name and nothing else (Acts 4:12). A lost first love weakens love for self, your wife, children, etc. The greatest

---

[3] Henry Scougal. *The Life of God in the Soul of Man*. Public Domain. The book can be accessed in PDF format:
http://www.ccel.org/s/scougal/life/cache/life.pdf (accessed October 10, 2017).

command to love God with our whole hearts, minds, souls, and strengths is the greatest because it directs us to the one thing in life that makes us the humans we ought and want to be. Loving God first and most enables us to love others. Loving self, first and most, harms us and others.

In particular, pornography is dehumanizing; it debases the image of God in both you and others, objectifies women as less than God created them to be, and isolates you from real relationships.

Sin refocused Adam and Eve's attention and affection. Moses repeatedly encouraged Israel to remember God (Deuteronomy 5:15), not to concentrate on their enemies (7:18). In effect, we become what we worship (Psalm 115:4-8). In the New Testament, James advises his readers to submit to God as the means of resisting sin (James 4:7). And Paul instructed the Thessalonians that genuine conversion was turning to God away from idols (1 Thessalonians 1:9), not vice versa.

THINK ABOUT IT

Attention to and affection for Jesus makes our souls excellent. A focus on sin or ensuing sorrow depresses our soul. Thinking on Jesus elevates our soul.

3

The Truth about Sex

Sex is a beautiful gift from God intended to enhance our pleasure and advance his kingdom on earth (Genesis 1:28). It originated in the divinely sanctified union of Adam and Eve and finds its greatest joy in that same covenant of marriage. As with all God's creation, there is no better way to enjoy it than as God ordained. Any deviation distorts, hence lessens and perhaps even destroys, the inherent blessing of the gift.

Genesis 2:24 reads: "Therefore a man shall leave his father and his mother and hold fast to his wife, and they shall become one flesh." That means

- Sex deepened the love relationship between Adam and Eve as they became "one flesh."
- This is God's plan for all marriages.

God made Eve out of Adam. They were male and female (Genesis 1:27), each a distinct and separate entity. In this way Adam and

Eve reflected the unity and diversity of God. Sex is intended to reunify what was originally one. In this way Adam and Eve reflected the unity and trinity of God. Your marriage was created to do the same.

God intends sex to unify a couple. Satan manipulates sex to disrupt a couple. The first visible result of Adam and Eve's sin was recognition of their disunity and shame (Genesis 3:7). It also cleaved them from God and ended in the death of a son. All sin ends in death, the death of honesty, relationship, even eternal death. Adam and Eve didn't just lose life forever in the garden; they lost the quality of life God intended for the garden.

If salvation is all about life, then sin is all about death. If salvation is all about unity, then sin is all about schism. If salvation is all about reconciliation, then sin is all about division. Pornography tears at the "one flesh" principle, ripping you from God and your wife as literally as your flesh being torn. Imagine that happening literally, the pain beyond imagination.

Sin splits us into two people; one public and one private person, the results of which are hypocrisy at best and eternal death at worst. If you can live in unrepentant sin, you are not a Christian. That is a harsh statement but true. Self-deception is perhaps sin's greatest ally. But the apostle of love, John, wrote:

"We know that everyone who has been born of God does not keep on sinning…" (1 John 5:18). You are only a Christian "if Christ is in you...[and] If the Spirit of him who raised Jesus from the dead dwells in you….[and] if by the Spirit you put to death the deeds of the body, you will live. For all [and only those] who are led by the Spirit of God are sons of God" (see Romans 8:10-14). Your relationship to your wife and others is important but all other relationships are secondary to your relationship to Jesus. More than this life is at stake.

Remorse, depression, and humiliation are the natural repercussions of guilt intended to drive you to repentance. Unmet by grace, sin will destroy you in every way and ultimately eternally. "Sin when it is fully grown," James teaches, "brings forth death" (James 1:15). No one initially appreciates conviction but conviction proves we are God's children. "For the moment all discipline seems painful rather than pleasant, but later it yields the peaceful fruit of righteousness to those who have been trained by it" (Hebrews 12:11).

As it did with Adam and as it has done so ever since, sin separates us from our most important relationships: God, ourselves, and then our wives. You know this is true. Christians involved in pornography don't pray, read the Bible, lead their wives or children in godliness or joyfully attend church. Pornography has also robbed you of the innocence of monogamy. It has shamed you into the isolation of secrecy. It has subdued your physical passion for your wife. Pornography has weakened every aspect of your spiritual and marital relationship.

And there is no such thing as victimless sin. You, your wife, even the women portrayed in pornography, suffer from its devastation. It seems for every good thing God created, Satan has a disastrous alternative. This is true of all sin, the exchange of treasure for trash. And like all sin, pornography has ever-increasing demands with ever-diminishing satisfaction. This sin hasn't stopped with pornography, has it? Its effect has exponentially multiplied, causing you to sin in other areas of your life, threatening everything valuable.

But just as Satan works to destroy the good that God created, the Lord is reconciling all things to himself through Christ (2 Corinthians 5:19 and Colossians 1:19-20). Reconciliation restores everything to its former glory and more. God is putting us back together as individuals. This is the real meaning of integrity, i.e., wholeness.

Grace restores our relationships with God and others. The gospel will eventually restore all creation and everything will be made new. Until then we all "groan inwardly as we wait eagerly for adoption as sons, the redemption of our bodies" (Romans 8:29), i.e., the consummation of our salvation. In the interim, you can be made whole and your relationships can be restored.

That renewal begins with the realization that sex is intended to exist between one man and one woman for a lifetime. It continues with the genuine repentance that leads to a change of mind, heart, and behavior. It is grounded in the Holy Spirit's application of personal, daily disciplines that train you in godliness (1 Timothy 4:7; 2 Timothy 3:16-17 and Titus 2:11-12).

THINK ABOUT IT

God intends sex to unify a couple. Satan manipulates sex to divide a couple.

4

Spiritual Transformation

Innumerable plans to overcome pornography center on our human ability to employ mechanistic strategies. We naïvely fill our lives with good things incapable of doing what only God can do. Those things quickly become sinful because they covertly divert our attention and affection from God. We may create more respectable idols but they are idols nonetheless. They are also incapable of creating the heart change necessary to biblically relate to God and others. In the process, we bring disrepute to good things and good people whom we abuse by granting them divine status. We and others end up worse for the wear.

Jesus taught the inadequacy of moral reformation. In Matthew 12:43-45 he recounted the story of a man possessed with a single demon who, through moral reformation, gained sufficient strength to overcome his sinning addiction. But the end result was the return of the demon with seven worse demons. The Lord lamented: "The last state of that person is worse than the first."

Nothing can replace God. Israel's great sin was twofold; they forsook God *and* created substitutes destined to fail and disappoint (Jeremiah 2:13). Without the Holy Spirit's enablement, every recourse will eventually fail and you will relapse into a worse condition as a result of depending on it.

At the same time, you must cooperate with God's work in your life. The Scripture repeatedly affirms appropriate planning (Luke 14:28). God does not bless laziness. Paul charged Timothy to "think over what I say" and to simultaneously realize that "the Lord will give you understanding…" (2 Timothy 2:7). In a very famous passage Paul exemplified this concept. He wrote: "I have been crucified with Christ. It is no longer I who live, but Christ who lives in me" (Galatians 2:20). His prayer was that he would "not nullify the grace of God" acting as though righteousness could be obtained by works. If so, "then Christ died for no purpose" (Galatians 2:21). The same is true of you. Change will not occur without your effort. But your efforts will not produce the necessary change.

The problem is not in our plans but our ultimate trust in them. Throughout the Old Testament God warned Israel not to trust in alliances with other nations. King David, the man who slew Goliath and understood the value of weaponry in battle, lamented that our tendency is to trust in chariots and horses rather than in God (Psalm 20:7). His son Solomon, who knew something about building temples, taught that "Unless the LORD builds the house, those who build it labor in vain. Unless the LORD watches over the city, the watchman stays awake in vain" (Psalm 127:1). The apostle Paul confessed that even "though we walk in the flesh, we are not waging war according to the flesh. [Instead] the weapons of our warfare are not of the flesh but have divine power to destroy strongholds" (2 Corinthians 10:3-4).

At the end of his second letter to the believers at Corinth, Paul commended his readers to "The grace of the Lord Jesus Christ and the love of God and the fellowship of the Holy Spirit…" (2 Corinthians 13:14). This is your offensive triad. God's unchanging love should motivate you to obey him. Christ's grace will give you a heart to do so. The Holy Spirit's fellowship will enable you.

Israel repeatedly failed to keep the covenants God graciously made with them. But instead of forsaking his people God promised them a new covenant, a future hope realized in Jesus. What did God promise? "And I will give you a new heart, and a new spirit I will put within you. And I will remove the heart of stone from your flesh and give you a heart of flesh. And I will put my Spirit within you, and cause you to walk in my statutes and be careful to obey my rules" (Ezekiel 36:26-27). This promise should form the basis of your prayers as you employ necessary practices to cooperate with the Trinity in love, grace, and fellowship.

THINK ABOUT IT

God's unchanging love should motivate you to obey him. Christ's grace will give you a heart to do so. The Holy Spirit's fellowship will enable you.

5

Ten Things about Pornography

You've been waiting for this list. We love lists. Our motto is "Just give me something to do and I'll do it." But never mistake busyness for God's business.

And remember, the ultimate goal of your plan is to love the Lord your God with all your heart and with all your soul and with your mind and with all your strength" (Mark 12:30). Only as you love God first and foremost will you correctly love yourself, your wife, your children or anybody else in your life. Anything else is something less and anything less will not, cannot, do what needs to be accomplished in your life.

So here it is. Don't show yourself any mercy. God will do that.

ONE

Acknowledge to yourself that pornography is sin. The man who "… conceals his transgressions will not prosper, but he who confesses and forsakes them will obtain mercy. [Contrarily,] Blessed is the one who fears the LORD always, but whoever hardens his heart will fall into calamity" (Proverbs 28:13-14). The Bible guarantees "your sin will find you out" (Numbers 32:23).

Sin has inescapable natural consequences. But you already know that. The sooner you acknowledge your sin, the sooner you can move on to steps 2-10 and into freedom.

Remember that trying to excuse your actions is not an acknowledgement of your sin. You may need to ask God to let you understand the horror of this sin before you can adequately confess it. When you do, don't offer any excuses. There is never any excuse for sin. Acknowledge to yourself that pornography is sin.

TWO

Don't blame anyone else. You alone are responsible for your sin. If you are married, your wife is not to blame. Her actions do not determine your actions. You alone are responsible to God for your life. You can't blame friends. You can't blame pressure at work. You can't blame a woman. You can't blame temptation. You can't even blame the devil.

God declares unequivocally that you, and you alone, are responsible for your sin. Ezekiel 18:20 declares "The soul who sins shall die." At the judgment seat of Christ, "each of us will give an account of himself to God" (Romans 14:10-12). You alone are to blame for your thoughts and actions. How perverse is sin? When confronted about his sin, Adam attempted to blame Eve and then God (Genesis 3:12). But Adam did not escape the consequences of his own sin. There is no one to blame but yourself.

THREE

Confess you sin to God. If you are married, confess your sin to your wife and to an accountability partner—in that order. Get on your knees right now and confess your sin to God. Don't excuse your sin. Confess it. Excusing it and confessing it are two different things.

If your wife isn't present, arrange a time to speak with her specifically and only about this. This won't be easy. Nothing worthwhile ever is.

It is impossible to imagine the hurt and emotion your wife will experience as you confess to her. There is no way to calculate her response. Of course, you want her to forgive you but you cannot control her immediate responses. But you are confessing your sin to her because you love God, because you love her, because you love your marriage, because you have sinned against her, and because it is the right thing to do before God. As you confess, don't make promises you can't or won't keep.

Be sure you pray for your wife before and after you speak to her. Afterward, make yourself available to her whenever she wants to discuss the matter. More could be said about this but this is why you need pastoral care for yourself and your wife. Your pastor will counsel you and your wife. He may even encourage you and your wife to confide in a Christian counselor.

FOUR

Find a male accountability partner after you speak with your wife, and ensure your wife and accountability partner can communicate about your faithfulness to an accountability relationship. Your accountability partner should be someone who is willing to walk with you through this situation and invest in a study on purity with you (the study will be suggested later). He must also be a person who is willing to ask you difficult questions and hold you accountable.

Arrange to meet with this person for the term of the study. When the study is completed, get another accountability partner for life and ongoing life issues. You should also regularly meet with a group of other men for study, fellowship, and accountability. Groups of men from your church regularly meet in times other than church hours. Find a group and join it. God dwells in eternal community. Jesus surrounded himself with men and women who loved him and cared for him (Matthew 26:6-13, 27:55; Mark 14:32-42; Luke

8:2-3). You should follow the same principle.

You got yourself into pornography. Don't trust yourself to get you out of it. You need the body of Christ. Specifically, you need someone to walk with you through a study on purity. This will replace sinful thoughts and behaviors with righteous ones and give the Holy Spirit time to retrain your mind and heart. The Psalmist asked: "How can a young man keep his way pure?" God's answer is: "By guarding it according to your word" (Psalm 119:9).

FIVE

Ask your wife to attend counseling with you. If she opts not to do so, go to counseling on your own. Call your pastor and arrange counseling. If you don't have a church home, call a pastor whom you know of or the pastor of a friend. You need biblically based counseling. Only God's word and God's Spirit can create lifelong change.

If you cannot find a pastor, which is highly unlikely, find a male Christian counselor. It is important to recognize that there is a difference between a counselor who is a Christian but counsels using secular methods, and a Christian counselor who employs the Bible to counsel. Choose the latter. The Bible is the power of God to save you (Romans 1:16) and sanctify you. (See Acts 20:32.)

When you meet with the pastor or counselor, confess everything. Unless he has been in the pastorate for less than a day, you won't surprise him. But if you are not honest, you will not reap the benefit of his counsel.

SIX

Create boundaries. This is how you "flee youthful passions and pursue righteousness, faith, love, and peace, along with those who call on the Lord from a pure heart" (2 Timothy 2:22). Get rid of any pornography in your possession, on your computer, etc., and disable your ability to access it.

Engage Internet software to ban pornography from any Internet accessible device you own. This probably already exists on your work computers. If not, ask your employer how a filter can be placed on all computers so that you can more effectively serve the company in the wisest use of your time. Ask your pastor for his suggestions about software programs. Ensure this software is active on any and all of your devices that can access the Internet.

Put any home computer screen where it can be viewed by anyone who walks by—in the kitchen, in your study, etc. Don't use a computer where the screen is visible only to you.

SEVEN

Depend on the Holy Spirit for transformation. You've already read this but it bears repeating. God informed Zechariah that personal or national weaknesses would not deter fulfillment of the Lord's plans. It's the same with you. Freedom will not be accomplished "by might, nor by power, but by my Spirit, says the LORD of hosts" (Zechariah 4:6).

Study the Word of God, memorize it, meditate on it, and ask God, by His Spirit, to work it out in your life. Start with Psalm 1:1-6 and Psalm 19:7-14. Don't just create a vacuum with abstinence from pornography. Sins of *omission* (a lack of Christian disciplines) lead to sins of *commission* such as pornography. Fill your heart and mind with God's word. Something will fill your mind, so make the choice for it to be the God's word.

Exclaim with the psalmist, "I will not set before my eyes anything that is worthless" (Psalm 101:3) and "I will meditate on your precepts and fix my eyes on your ways. I will delight in your statutes; I will not forget your word" (Psalm 119:15-16). Those are also two good verses to memorize in your fight with sin.

If you don't already have a Bible reading plan, find one and begin to employ it daily. I could recommend one for you but asking your pastor about one will enhance your relationship with him.

EIGHT

First thing every morning, make the conscious decision to "put off your old self, which belongs to your former manner of life and is corrupt through deceitful desires, and to be renewed in the spirit of your minds, and to put on the new self, created after the likeness of God in true righteousness and holiness" (Ephesians 4:22-24). This is a daily choice. Do it every day. How do you do this?

Wake up every day and say, "Lord Jesus, I can't live the Christian life. But you lived it perfectly and your Spirit now lives in me. I surrender to you. Live your life in me."

Then enact the disciplines that Jesus practiced in order to follow him. To follow Jesus means to follow Jesus' life. If you were a first-century disciple following him, what would your life look like? You would talk to him; that's prayer. You would listen to him; that's Bible study. You would work with him serving others. The disciplines of the Christian life would make a great second study after your study on purity.

NINE

Pornography is a private sin—something you do alone and in secrecy. To counter its covert environment, get regularly involved in church and a small group. This is a biblical pattern for Christian living. Jesus faithfully attended the synagogue (Luke 2:42, 4:16) and also surrounded himself with a small group of friends we know as the disciples.

Commit to live your life transparently with others. You will discover that the Bible is true when it says, "No temptation has taken you that is not common to man" (1 Corinthians 10:13). People will be encouraged by your life and will find encouragement in the stories of other people. It's true that "Two are better than one…" (Ecclesiastes 4:9). Living life with others is the way God intends you to live. The natural benefits of doing so are innumerable.

TEN

Don't do shortcuts. There are none. Do the hardest things and this will yield the most meaningful results. Don't think you can shortcut the cure to pornography. Sin will kill you or you will kill it. In Colossians 3:5, the apostle Paul counsels you to "Put to death therefore what is earthly in you: sexual immorality, impurity, passion, evil desire, and covetousness, which is idolatry." The flesh doesn't want to die. It will protest. It is natural to live sinfully but supernatural to live godly. Living after the flesh reaps destruction and death. Godliness reaps abundant life now and eternal life forever. (See Romans 7:24-25 and 8:8-14.)

Addictions take time to build and recovery takes time to construct. It is an everyday process. You will have to rebuild trust with your wife and perhaps with other people. This will take time. It may take time for your wife or others to forgive you. Counseling will take time. It will take time to install the essential precautions that will keep you from pornography and to build the necessary disciplines that positively influence your life. But each step you take toward godliness is a step toward freedom from pornography.

THINK ABOUT IT

The ultimate goal of your plan is to love the Lord your God with all your heart, and with all your soul, and with your mind, and with all your strength (Mark 12:30).

6

Questions and Answers

It is important to state that this book is intended to offer initial direction. You undoubtedly have questions so this section provides a synopsis of commonly asked questions.

Is pornography really adultery?

Yes. Jesus stated, "You have heard that it was said, 'You shall not commit adultery.' But I say to you that everyone who looks at a woman with lustful intent has already committed adultery with her in his heart" (Matthew 5:27-28). Pornography is a textbook definition of adultery.

Should I tell my wife?

Absolutely. As soon as possible, but in the proper circumstances. Godliness means honoring your wife (1 Peter 3:7). Your wife is your flesh. You and she are one. Transparency is the soil of sanctification. Sin thrives in secrecy. You are responsible to live in truth with her and "truth in love" (Ephesians 4:15) will mature both of you. In reality, your wife knows something is wrong and you do not want to be caught attempting to hide your sin. It will only decrease the chances for reconciliation.

Your wife loves you more than anyone. That's why your confession will hurt her more than anyone else. This is also why she will commit herself to your restoration. Responses to such a revelation vary from person to person. Your confession will deeply pierce your wife's heart and her self-esteem.

Be willing to answer all of her questions. Don't hide anything. Feel her hurt. Don't tell her how she should feel or try to direct her emotions. Give her the time and opportunity to reflect. Recognize that time is required to rebuild her trust. But before you part after the initial conversation, assure her of your repentance before God, your desire to live a godly life, and the practical steps you have taken and will take to regain the Lord's blessing and her trust.

Most importantly, pray for your wife before you share this devastating news, and continue to pray for her.

What if my wife seeks separation or divorce?

Your obedience must be independent of your wife's choices. Live proactively, not reactively. Obey God because you love God. Don't make your feelings, happiness or your wife's responses an idol. Love God first and most. In addition, your love for your wife should remain unconditional, an expression of God's love for you and through you. This is how God loves you. God gave you to her to love her as he loves her (Ephesians 5:25f). This is one of the reasons your sin hurts her so much. One aspect of your recovery is the commitment to model Christ's love for her.

Should we seek counseling?

Absolutely and as soon as possible. Pornography is not the root issue. Its motivations are deep-seated and most often invisible, even unknown to its participant. Freedom is dependent on discovering and uprooting them, then creating new disciplines to redirect your mind, heart, and behaviors.

Your marriage can survive but only if you and your wife are committed to loving Christ first and foremost. She will need counseling and perhaps her own accountability partner. Your sin raises innumerable issues for her. Don't delay. Make arrangements for counseling today. If your wife is unwilling to attend counseling, go alone.

And again, remember there is a difference between a Christian who counsels and Christian counseling. Choose Christian counseling.

Should I have an accountability partner?

Yes. Pornography is a sin you've committed alone. The rescue is accomplished in tandem. Your heart is so deceitful and desperately wicked that you can't know it (Jeremiah 17:9). Recovery requires a new, objective set of eyes to recognize pride, cultivate humility, restore brokenness, and eliminate idols—all essential resources for success. If you don't know anyone who has proven worthy of your trust, speak to your pastor and ask him to help you locate someone in whom you can confide

This person should be willing to regularly meet with you, ask you hard questions, lead you in a Bible study about holiness, pray for you, and be available to you when needed. If she desires, your wife should also have access to this person. She may want to occasionally contact this person to validate your progress. Of course, ongoing meetings with this individual will subside over time. But initially set something practical for both of your schedules. Also, set a deadline for the strict accountability in which you are entering, perhaps for the length of the study I will suggest.

In addition, you should have an accountability partner for the rest of your life. This is someone with whom you regularly meet, preferably weekly at the least, for prayer, truth-telling, and the encouragement of Scripture.

To whom should I confess this sin?

The extent of your confession should encompass the range of your sin. You need to confess this sin to your wife. In addition, however, you need an accountability partner, and a pastor or counselor. You must confess your sin to them so that they have the information needed to best help you. Beyond that, you should only involve those people necessary to the reconciliation process. This may include your pastor and a friend with whom your wife can confide.

You might also enlist a support group of men who meet to combat pornography. Such groups do exist. Your pastor is an excellent resource to help you locate a group like this. Your sin is serious and should be dealt with accordingly but your goal is reconciliation with God and others, not embarrassment or punishment. Include only trusted advisors who will work with you toward that end.

What study do you suggest?

There are many valuable resources but I highly suggest *Setting Capitives Free: The Way of Purity* by Mike Cleveland. It's published by Focus Publishing in Bemidji, Minnesota, and is available on Amazon. It is an intensive study but pornography is an insidious sin deeply driven into a man's soul. It will not be easily uprooted and new disciplines will not be easily incorporated.

Stephen Arterburn's *Every Man's Battle: Winning the War on Sexual Purity One Victory at a Time* is also a good resource.

In militaristic, warfaring terms the apostle Paul said, "We destroy arguments and every lofty opinion raised against the knowledge of God, and take every thought captive to obey Christ, being ready to punish every disobedience, when your obedience is complete" (2 Corinthians 10:5-6). Couple that verse with 1 Corinthians 9:26-27 which reads "So I do not run aimlessly; I do not box as one beating the air. But I discipline my body and keep it under control, lest after preaching to others I myself should be disqualified." These are two more verses you should memorize. They give you a sense of the gravity with which you should take your Christianity, a seriousness required to live a godly life.

Should I employ Internet protection software?

For the rest of your life. Digital rules should rule your relationship to the Internet. As mentioned earlier, no computer screen in your home should face a private wall but be oriented toward the open space of a room so that anyone can see the monitor. Of course cell phones and iPads complicate the matter but IPSs can be employed for all of these devices. This may include but is not limited to filtering software, hardware filters, and Internet proxy filters.

Investigate Covenant Eyes which blocks Internet Porn. The software X3Watch tracks your Internet usage and sends a record of objectionable sites to an accountability partner of your choosing.

You should regularly assess why and how you are accessing technology. Is it for work? Does it build your faith and testimony? Are you devoting sufficient time to other activities that create health for you? In the digital age, it is easy to justify an inordinate use of the Internet. This is something you should discuss with your wife, pastor, and accountability partner.

What if my wife wants constant access to my phone and other electronic devices?

She should have complete access to any Internet device you possess and you should have equal access to her devices. In addition, you should both know all the passwords for every

Internet device. It is a rare occasion for a man or woman to a work in an environment that demands secrecy from a spouse.

Are there particular spiritual disciplines that will enable me to succeed?

Yes. You can train yourself to godliness (1 Timothy 4:7-8). Scripture memorization is essential. Psalm 119:11 reads: "I have stored up your word in my heart, that I might not sin against you." God's hidden word provides the track for omnipotence in the person of the Holy Spirit and enables you to live righteously. Immediately begin memorizing Psalm 101:3a. Say the reference, the verse, and repeat the reference. Then memorize 1 Corinthians 9:26-27 and 2 Corinthians 10:5-6. Place the verse on an index card, post-it note or make it your screensaver on your phone. Make memorization a lifestyle choice. The Navigators have a proven *Topical Memory System* and Desiring God Ministries offers *Fighter Verses* at http://fighterverses.com/the-verses/fighter-verses/. There are also memorization APPS.

A daily devotional time that incorporates Bible reading, prayer, and memorization is essential to a well-built Christian life. God speaks to you in the Bible and you talk to God in prayer. Such communication is essential for the success of any relationship. Spurgeon's *Morning and Evening* is a perfect devotional book. But you should also study with others. The small groups of a church setting provide an atmosphere conducive to spiritual growth. Don't let shyness keep you from spirituality. It could be pride, masquerading as humility.

THINK ABOUT IT

Your marriage can survive but only if
you and your wife are committed to
loving Christ first and foremost.

7

Practical Pointers

This section is dedicated to helping you work through the many points of this book. I'm a visual learner and I appreciate maps. I hope this part will enable you to see what needs to be done, that you have done it, and rejoice in the progress you are making. This tool will help you, your wife, and your accountability partner to know that you are holding yourself accountable for life change.

However, before I present you with the planner, I want to tell you how your life is going to change. This is important because knowing how you succeed gives you a road map for future success. In particular, Philippians 2:13 is the road map for success in your fight with pornography.

The apostle Paul wrote the letter to the Philippians to encourage a Roman audience to prize their heavenly citizenship above their Roman nationality. This was a difficult request from Paul. The city of Philippi had earned its Roman heritage. Its citizenry was comprised of retired and honored soldiers, many of them veterans of Caesar's own Praetorian Guard. Many others of them were initially defeated foreigners, conscripted into Rome's service. But together, their service to Rome had won them the leisure of retirement and freedom, even Roman citizenship with all of its ensuing benefits.

Paul wasn't asking them to reform an army and fight against Rome. He was simply asking them to live out their Christianity in the midst of a pagan Philippi. This meant honoring Christian virtues the Romans considered vices, particularly those of humility and servanthood. In chapter two, Paul asks them particularly to

> Do nothing from selfish ambition or conceit, but in humility count others more significant than yourselves. Let each of you look not only to his own interests, but also to the interests of others.

He then presents Jesus as the ultimate model of this lifestyle (2:5-12) and encourages them to "work out [their] own salvation with fear and trembling…" (2:12). How were the proud, undefeated, most dominant force of men on the planet supposed to follow Jesus to the cross of humility and servanthood?

Thankfully, the letter doesn't end there. Paul doesn't leave them to figure it out on their own. He not only tells them what to do—live humbly and as a servant—but also how to do it. Remember, what he's asking goes against every fiber in their Roman conquering bodies. Consider as the apostle informs these Romans how to "be blameless and innocent, children of God without blemish in the midst of a crooked and twisted generation…" (2:15). He writes in verse 13, "for [working out their salvation in humility and servanthood] it is God who works in you, both to will and to work for his good pleasure."

This is Paul's prescription for holiness in the midst of an unholy world. It is also the means by which you will live a holy life in a world that is constantly tugging at your heart for its allegiance.

Paul's battle plan for victory (to use the Roman's way of thinking) is a twofold strategy: God works in you both (a) to will and (b) to work for his good pleasure. Do you see it? It is God who gives you the desire and the ability to please him. Thankfully, God does not leave it to you. His Holy Spirit, an equal member of the Trinity with the Father and the Son, dwells in you to please him.

Think about the Father's power. He created everything that exists. Think about Jesus' power. He healed the sick, ruled nature, and even raised the dead. Think about the Holy Spirit's power. He raised Jesus from the dead and resurrects the hearts of dead sinners to repent and believe on Jesus for salvation.

Does this remove your responsibility? Absolutely not! You have to cooperate with God's will for your holiness by obeying the word, enacting prayer as a discipline, making yourself accountable, removing temptation, replacing sin with righteous habits, and live repenting as you sin, etc.

Philippians 2:13 gives you courage and hope by reminding you that even though you fight the battle, God will give you the victory. Even as I write this, I'm thinking about Israel whom God called to take the Promised Land. The book of Joshua records Israel's military conflicts with the nations who occupied the Promised Land. It concludes with the words "Thus the LORD gave to Israel all the land that he swore to give to their fathers. And they took possession of it, and they settled there" (Joshua 21:43). Did you see Philippians 2:13 in that verse? "The LORD gave to Israel all the land that he swore…" and "they took possession of it…"

In this section of *Practical Pointers* I am suggesting you keep a record of your battle plan so that you can know what needs to be done, what you have accomplished, and what you have yet to do. But in it all, remember, it is God who is giving you both the will and the ability to do these things.

When you lack the will to do a hard thing, ask God for the grace of a willing heart to obey. He will encourage you. He will enable you.

Paul knew from firsthand experience what he was asking of the Philippians. He had learned the hard way that God's "grace is sufficient for you, for my power is made perfect in weakness" (2 Corinthians 12:9). He didn't write the Philippians in an impersonal vacuum but out of his own personal experiences. Consider 2 Corinthians 4:7-11:

> But we have this treasure in jars of clay, to show that the surpassing power belongs to God and not to us. We are afflicted in every way, but not crushed; perplexed, but not driven to despair; persecuted, but not forsaken; struck down, but not destroyed; always carrying in the body the death of Jesus, so that the life of Jesus may also be manifested in our bodies.

- You are a jar of clay (v. 7a)
- that demonstrates God's surpassing power (v. 7b)
- no matter the affliction (vv. 8-9a)

- you will not be forsaken or destroyed (v. 9b)
- so that Jesus' life may be demonstrated in you (v. 10b)

God is asking you to do something that doesn't come naturally; it's supernatural. God is requiring a supernatural life of a normal person but he is also promising that he will enable you to live that life so that you experience and others around you witness his saving, sanctifying grace.

Know this: there is simply no excuse for sin. Wherever and however strong sin may be, God's grace "abounds all the more" (Romans 5:20).

Memorize Philippians 2:13, 2 Corinthians 12:9, 2 Corinthians 4:7-11, and Romans 5:20. God will use these Scriptures to create meaningful, lasting change in your life.

Spending time in God's word, fellowshipping with your accountability partner or other Christians, investing the time in your wife (and children), as well as serving God at your local church and in community projects will also fill the void of time created by eliminating pornography. These good habits will help you "put off the old self with its practices" and "put on the new self, which is being renewed in knowledge after the image of its creator" (Colossians 3:9-10).

Remember, shortcuts will cut short any progress. With all of that in mind, here are the *Practical Pointers*, the battle plan for victory.

THINK ABOUT IT

God is asking you to do something that doesn't come naturally; it's supernatural. God is requiring a supernatural life of a normal person but he is also promising that he will enable you to live that life.

8

Action Review Checklist

1 Before God, I have repented of and not excused the sin of pornography.
- ☐ Yes
- ☐ No

2 I have rid myself of any available pornography.
- ☐ Yes
- ☐ No

3 I have placed appropriate Internet protection software on all my devices.
- ☐ Yes
- ☐ No

4 I have prayed for my wife.
- ☐ Yes
- ☐ No

5 I have confessed this sin to my wife without excuse or reservation and asked for her forgiveness, allowing her to ask questions of me.
- ☐ Yes
- ☐ No

6 My wife has complete access to all of my Internet devices.
- ☐ Yes
- ☐ No

7 I have contacted a pastor for an appointment.
- ☐ Yes
- ☐ No

The pastor's name is

_____

Appointment date and time

_____

I have prayed for the pastor before my initial visit.
- ☐ Yes
- ☐ No

8 I have kept my appointment with the pastor.
- ☐ Yes
- ☐ No

9 I have contacted a counselor for myself and/or my wife.
- ☐ Yes
- ☐ No

Appointment date and time

_____

The counselor's name is

_____

I have prayed for the counselor before my initial visit.
- ☐ Yes
- ☐ No

10 I have kept my initial counseling appointment.
- ☐ Yes
- ☐ No

11 I have made an appointment with a potential accountability partner.
- ☐ Yes
- ☐ No

Appointment time and date

_____

12 I have kept my initial appointment with my accountability partner.
- ☐ Yes
- ☐ No

13 My accountability partner's name is

_____

14 My accountability partner and I are going to meet (how often, when and where)

_____

_____

15 I have ordered the study *Setting Captives Free: The Way of Purity* or another appropriate study.
- ☐ Yes
- ☐ No

16 My accountability partner and I are doing the study.
- ☐ Yes
- ☐ No

17 These are the Bible verses I have and am memorizing:

_____

_____

_____

18 Here is a list of things I am doing with my time and a list of new habits I am employing to invest my mind, heart, and body in God's kingdom: my marriage, my church, and my community.

_____

_____

_____

_____

_____

_____

There is simply no way to list all of the practical suggestions you will need or engage as you experience God's grace in your victory campaign against pornography. Your wife, pastor, and accountability partner may offer other suggestions. Room has been provided below this paragraph for you to write those down and keep track of God's good work in you.

_____

_____

_____

_____

Now to him who is able to keep you from stumbling and to present you blameless before the presence of his glory with great joy, to the only God, our Savior, through Jesus Christ our Lord, be glory, majesty, dominion, and authority, before all time and now and forever. Amen.
(Jude 24-25)

9

Conclusion

You are not alone. Jesus, who is your supreme advocate, was tempted in every way but without sin (Hebrews 4:15). His sinless response to temptations makes him the perfect friend and counselor.

Others have walked this journey before you. They will make themselves available to you and you will learn much from them.

Your wife is your closest human companion. She loves you. She will no doubt be hurt by the revelation of this addiction but she is your best friend and, as the Holy Spirit enables her, and greatest ally and most influential accountability partner.

One last thought. It will be beneficial for your wife to read this book. It will demonstrate the repentance that has driven you to seek help and the steps you are taking to heal your life and marriage. It will also help her to rest in the knowledge that every day is moving your marriage one day further from this particular sin and the hurt it has caused. You and she can also repeatedly refer to it as you complete the *Practical Pointers* section.

Finally, the prize is certainly worth the effort. We are promised "fullness of joy" with Jesus (Psalm 16:11). Nothing can compare to the Christian life. As you journey toward knowing and loving God, your life will be transformed. And one day, you will hear Christ himself say, "Well done, good and faithful servant" (Matthew 25:21).

About the Author

REGGIE WEEMS is married to his childhood sweetheart, Teana. They share three children and nine grandchildren. He has pastored two congregations: the first for ten years and the second since 1991. He also teaches theology, Bible, and humanities at two universities. His DMin in Pastoral Leadership and Management is from Liberty University, and his PhD in Historical Theology is from the University of Babes-Bolyai in Cluj-Napoca, Romania.

www.10thingsabout.org

To buy quantities of this book at a special rate for bulk use, email info@greatwriting.org

www.ingramcontent.com/pod-product-compliance
Lightning Source LLC
Chambersburg PA
CBHW070548300426
44113CB00011B/1829